65p

*Discovery Methods
in Physical Education*

NELSON'S TEACHER TEXTS

Forthcoming Titles

BASIC DESIGN IN WOOD

THE TEACHING OF ENGLISH TO LINGUISTICALLY
DEPRIVED CHILDREN

SPEECH TRAINING

NELSON'S TEACHER TEXTS

Discovery Methods
in Physical Education

JOHN COPE

*Principal Lecturer and Head of Department
of Physical Education,
Cheshire College of Education, Alsager*

NELSON

THOMAS NELSON AND SONS LTD
36 Park Street London W1
P.O. Box 2187 Accra
P.O. Box 336 Apapa Lagos
P.O. Box 25012 Nairobi
P.O. Box 21149 Dar es Salaam
77 Coffee Street San Fernando Trinidad

THOMAS NELSON (AUSTRALIA) LTD
597 Little Collins Street Melbourne C1

THOMAS NELSON AND SONS (SOUTH AFRICA) (PROPRIETARY) LTD
P.O. Box 7331 Johannesburg

THOMAS NELSON AND SONS (CANADA) LTD
81 Curlew Drive Don Mills Ontario

THOMAS NELSON AND SONS
Copewood and Davis Streets Camden New Jersey 08103

—

Second impression 1969

17 423050 8

PRINTED AND BOUND IN ENGLAND BY
HAZELL WATSON AND VINEY LTD
AYLESBURY, BUCKS

CONTENTS

1 Learning in the Gymnasium   1

2 Activity Development   16

3 Quantitative Development of Gymnastic Activity   21

4 Qualitative Development of Gymnastic Activity   39

5 A Summary and Suggestions for Recording the Lessons   54

6 The Senior Phase of Gymnastics   60

7 Determination to Learn   67

8 Organization   70

    Conclusion   82

CHAPTER ONE

Learning in the Gymnasium

Young children seem to express the joy of living by the exuberance of their movements. They move their bodies at every opportunity during work and play. An awareness of the capabilities of their bodies will have been derived from the handling of objects, from activities on hard and soft surfaces and on walls and in trees, from the management of their own bodies in many situations, and from supporting and contacting the weight of other children.

Unfortunately the opportunity for freedom of movement for children is decreasing. They need freedom from restriction to express and enjoy their physical skill, but gardens become smaller and green and wooded areas become more remote; fences and 'Keep Out' notices become accepted barriers to adventure. Games demanding physical skill and vigour are replaced by less active forms of recreation. The instinctive urge for physical challenge and experimentation is being curtailed in modern society. 'Good' behaviour, quiet and non-active pastimes, busy streets, and the increasing importance of certificates in education are but a few of the pressures restricting the physical experience of the child. Parents no longer look with pride on the physical prowess of their children but do their best to replace it with 'more rewarding' or at least 'less troublesome' occupations. As the population multiplies and physical restrictions continue to increase the gymnasium is likely to become more and more important as a place where children can still enjoy climbing, swinging, jumping, rolling, and balancing activities.

Is lack of skill in movement due to lack of opportunity rather than lack of ability? It is thought that deprivation of experience may delay maturation and if this experience is withheld at a critical stage in development then there may be a permanent lowering of level of performance. The less agile child is likely to be the one who has not had the opportunity at home or at play to run and jump and swing with other children. Parents may have placed barriers of safety and convention around their child and continually helped him in manipulative skills and bodily actions which should have provided experiences necessary for future learning. These children may continue to be restricted in their movements and in their attitude towards physical activities, simply because they have never had sufficient practice. Variation in physical attainment can be accounted for partly by lack of opportunity for experimental play and not entirely by heredity, maturity or somatotype.

The traditional gymnastic lesson did not take into account the variation in level of physical experience of children and the skill threshold demanded rarely fell below that attainable by the average child. Movement experience was restricted to selected skills and for some children the skill requested was in advance of, or behind the stage of motor learning which they had reached.

The progressive teacher of physical education has left restrictive practices behind and his lesson provides the opportunity for each child to extend his activity experience at his own level of ability. Set progressions have given way to experimentation. The teacher provides an environment which allows the child to follow his own lines of progression as his needs become apparent. Direct teaching has given way to intelligent guidance. The role of the teacher is now recognized as one in which he provides the child with the opportunity for learning and the traditional role of one who imparts information has diminished. His main function is to control the interaction between child and environment, e.g.

1 The teacher, through the environment, originates the work and provides appropriate experiences.
2 The child discovers facts and extends his knowledge with

help from the teacher and group, and he adopts an active approach to learning.

3 Achievement and progress is at an individual level.

4 Success is dependent on the teacher's ability to link the child's existing knowledge with the environmental circumstances, and on the attitude of the child to the learning situation.

Progressiveness in education is therefore based on the way in which the child learns rather than on techniques of teaching. How the child learns and why he learns, or does not learn, is as important to the educational philosophy of the teacher as specialization in a subject. Teaching methods should originate initially from the approach of the child to learning rather than being applied to the child; they are child-centred and not subject-centred.

The fundamental principle of helping the child to think and discover for himself is, of course, not new. For centuries past there have been advocates of child-centred education. Unfortunately information from historical sources has been looked upon as the 'Philosophy of Education' and there is a tendency not to connect philosophy with practice. Even up-to-date information advanced by research psychologists concerning the theories of learning is ignored by many teachers. They do not wish to change their approach to teaching, or do not see the relevance between the problems of their gymnasium and the problems of learning reported in other environments.

The first principle on which teaching is based is to start from what the child already knows and lead him into the unknown. The existing knowledge which a child has in a subject is called his schema and forms a structure into which new knowledge is integrated. The rate of learning and the use to which the child may put the newly acquired knowledge is dependent on the relationship between the existing schema and the problems posed by the environment. When the gap is too great rote-learning takes place which gives isolated knowledge. Generalizations are not possible unless 'dawn breaks' at a later stage, which sometimes happens with the intelligent child. True learning follows a pattern of experimentation and discovery in which the child uses his present knowledge to search for further information. Information is selected and clarified and his existing knowledge is revised and adjusted so that the information may be absorbed. The new knowledge may now be assimilated into the schema which is enlarged and adjusted and evaluated.

If a teacher is to present his subject in such a way that generalization should take place, he needs to be aware of the concepts involved in the subject and their interrelationship. A concept is not a fact but a set of experiences which have one thing, the concept, in common. Although learning patterns may vary from one child to another, concept building should follow a logical pattern if the knowledge is to be of use. A child should not be expected to learn a higher-order concept until the low-order concepts have been experienced, reflected upon, and related. He may learn isolated facts and use them in a narrow way but will not be able to recognize their relationship with problems that are somewhat different. I suggest that many of the traditional ideas upon which the teaching of physical education is based involve the learning of secondary concepts before primary concepts have been experienced and established.

The problem of 'structure' has been raised in the fields of reading and mathematics and is spreading to all subjects.

What is the fundamental structure of physical education? What are the primary concepts involved? Must we change our ideas of what is difficult for a child and what is a basic experience? At what age should we introduce specialization?

Research into the structure of P.E. could lead to far-reaching changes in the teaching of physical education.

Consideration of the structure of physical education leads to the suggestion of three hypotheses:

1 that a wide range of movements of the type experienced in free play and in dance and educational gymnastics are necessary for the formation of the primary concepts of physical education;

4

2 that analysis of movement is the symbolism which equips the child with a basic structure of knowledge from which he is able to generalize the strategies of problem-solving when faced with physical tasks;

3 that secondary concepts, consisting of physical skills which are fairly complex and limited to a specific environment, are more likely to be successfully and independently handled by a child if points one and two have been satisfactorily assimilated.

Research and a great deal of thought are necessary if physical education is not to become a second-class subject relegated to extracurricular or leisure-time programmes. A teacher needs to know whether there are critical stages in the growth and development of a child when certain movement experiences are necessary and if the 'Law of Readiness' applies to some movements before others. Is there, for example, a physiological age at which movements on the hands are easy to learn? If not experienced to some degree at this stage has the child decreased his potential, interest in, and his ability to learn these movements for the future? When one attempts to analyse activities and skills in terms of concepts, one is faced with many questions which are at present unanswerable.

Having looked briefly into effective learning the methods of teaching can be evaluated. For discussion purposes it is possible to separate teaching into three approaches which may be termed authoritarian, free environmental discovery, and directed discovery.

Authoritarian Teaching

The main criticism of authoritarian methods is that all activities are planned and developed by the teacher. He selects what he thinks is a suitable activity and sets out to teach it. It is demonstrated and everyone attempts to do the same activity in the same way at the same time. Some of the boys soon accomplish the skill and reach a fair standard. Others struggle and achieve some success but not the quality of performance. The remainder may never achieve anything worth while and their efforts receive no reward. Telling a boy exactly what to do is a negative form of teaching and should be used discreetly. Because direction allows no opportunity for exploration and discovery, independence of thought is not encouraged, and there is often a lack of understanding of *how* to tackle a physical task.

When gymnastics is taught by authoritarian methods the incentives to learn arise largely through teacher motivation. Good teaching and friendly relations with the class may result in a satisfactory standard of work in the lower secondary age-range. However, the adoption of rigid trial and error behaviour and the premature teaching of complex skills may lead to lack of interest, resistance to learning, and avoidance behaviour in the upper secondary age-range. A disappointed teacher may then adopt a more authoritarian and less friendly approach in an attempt to keep up the standard of work and this may eventually provoke open opposition to the subject. Direct teaching of gymnastics cannot often be used as a method applicable to the whole of the class. It does not cater for individual differences and cannot be justified educationally.

Physical skills taught in this way will probably have a linear growth and the majority of the class may not have sufficient breadth of experience to tackle a complex and demanding skill. The pyramidal type of experience arising from a permissive atmosphere may be necessary before they are able to restructure and modify their learning and gain understanding and insight into the problems involved in the performance of a new skill.

Environmental Discovery

Here the teacher provides a stimulating environment and allows freedom of activity. A bias towards this approach is used at Infant and lower Junior levels. The class works quite freely and its natural interest and curiosity in physical activity provides the learning situation. The first environmental stimuli arise from the floor and the space around. Simple problems are posed which can be answered by natural movement. The class is then confronted by the gymnastic apparatus and similar problems are posed.

This presents additional challenges and demands a wider interpretation and further experiment.

This method of presentation is a useful teaching technique at
what may be termed basic experience levels. The child is largely
self-motivated and works at his own level according to his interests,
ability, and previous experience. It is often used to encourage
experimentation and variation. However, if it is to be really
useful it must not become free activity with the exclusion of
teaching. Unsuitable and discouraging patterns of movement
must be guided into meaningful and enjoyable responses so that
the child recognizes that he is improving and learns *how* to
practise in order to improve. Set patterns of movement which
have brought early success may be repeated continually. This
should be discouraged. The child should be willing to respond to
the teacher and ready to change his approach and his movements
so that he is continually searching for more appropriate, more
successful, and more challenging movements.

This is a difficult method to use for any length of time without
the lessons becoming rather aimless. The teacher will find that
discovery leads to communication, communication leads to a
flow of information between teacher and class, which leads to
guidance. Environmental discovery which is largely unguided
may lead children to inefficient and unsuitable movements.
Discovery plus guidance is likely to be of more value to the child
educationally.

Directed Discovery

Directed discovery does not mean that the teacher tells the child
how to solve the problem, but that he helps the child towards an
appropriate answer by questions and suggestions. Having
arranged the environmental circumstances and set the task, he
helps the child to discover an appropriate answer by an effective
route. The teaching contains a sensible degree of guidance;
sensible in that it is related to the experience, the interest, and the
ways of learning of the pupil. Excessive guidance may cause

resistance to learning; too little guidance may cause interest to be lost and confidence weakened. The difficulty then is to assess the degree of direction which is most appropriate to the learning situation for each pupil. One needs teaching experience which involves close child contact to decide when to allow him to practise freely, when to limit his activity, and when to leave him to find out. Knowledge of children is necessary before one can successfully set the problems and pose the appropriate questions to stimulate a wide range of movement at all levels of ability.

The way in which the teacher helps each child should indicate his knowledge of his ability. In physical education it seems that a permissive atmosphere tends to help the able child and a slightly more directive one the less-able and timid child, a situation which perhaps differs from the academic subjects. The less-able children are helped by the security which is given by some guidance at the beginning of the learning situation and having started them off, the teacher may proceed to questioning for further guidance. As the child is challenged by more difficult situations it is to be expected that errors will occur and failure will be met. The child should develop the ability to accept a failure and continue with the practice or work out another method of approach. A failure should not be a defeat. The teacher has the task of making the reasons for errors understandable so that insight is gained and the same error is not committed again. The objective is a lesson in which achievement is possible for every member of the class, achievement which follows understanding and results from hard work.

If teaching method is evaluated with understanding and interest as the criteria, the directed discovery approach is superior to the alternative methods. This is particularly so in school gymnastics. When the teacher understands the educational basis of the approach he will find the gymnastic lesson easier to present. It is difficult to give a theoretical explanation of how a gymnastic lesson may develop from a natural activity to the many variations, sequences and movement experiences which arise in answer to questions or requests posed by the teacher. Perhaps the best means of illustration would be to supply a list of the type of questions which could be used to stimulate active learning. The questions are grouped into sections which tend to be directed towards an awareness of one factor of movement, i.e. parts of the body, time, weight or force, space, and sequences which stress two or more of these factors. They are not in a logical order for teaching purposes and are to be considered only as an example of presentation.

ROLLING

(a) Which parts are you using to roll on?

Which is the first part to touch the ground, the second, the last?

Can you change the order in which you use parts; reverse the order?

Can you find different parts on which to roll?

How do you start, and finish?

Are both sides of your body equally important?

Show me a roll in which one side of your body is the most important.

Can you roll from one side of your body to the other?

Can you roll without using your limbs?

Use the same body-parts as your partner but do a different roll.

Can you roll one half of your body while the other half is still?

(b) Can you roll quickly?

Show me a slow roll.

Find rolls which change between fast and slow.

Can you change speed during your roll?

Can you accelerate during a roll; during successive rolls?

Can you decelerate?

(c) Which rolls are difficult to do lightly?

Show me a roll in which you use part of your body in a strong manner.

Which parts are working hard and which parts only assist?

Can you roll carefully; vigorously?

(d) Show me rolls which take you directly to a selected spot.
Show me rolls which take you all over the floor.
Show a sequence of direct and roundabout rolling.
Can you roll in different directions?
Show a sequence which shows different shapes and different directions.
Show the difference between rolls which spread your body out and which close it in.
Can you show a sequence of rolls which include twisting, bending, and stretching?

(e) Show a sequence which clearly demonstrates that you know the different body-parts you can use while rolling in different directions.
In the above sequence, can you make one roll fast and another slow?
Show that you know where to start, where to travel, and where to finish.

JUMPING AND LANDING

(a) How are you using your feet?
Can you use your legs in a different way?
Which part initiates the jump?
Which parts are important?
Show a jump which makes equal use of the sides of your body; use one side only.
Can you show a sequence of jumps in which you take-off in different ways?
Which part goes the highest?
Make a different part go high.

(b) Is your preparation for the jump quick or slow?
Experiment with slow and quick preparations, from standing; using an approach.
Show me a sustained landing.
Can you land and assume a still position very quickly?
Show me a jump with a quick preparation and a slow landing.

(c) What is the shape of your body during the jump; during the landing?

Can you show other shapes?

Can you show a change of shape during the jump: retain a shape without the jump?

Show a sequence of jumps which demonstrate different shapes.

Can you jump in different directions?

(d) Show three jumps which use different body-parts and demonstrate different shapes. Link them into a sequence.

Show a sequence of jumps in which the landings are different.

Copy a sequence performed by your partner.

Can you combine with your partner in a jumping sequence?

RUNNING

(a) Which part of your foot do you use?

Where does your knee start/finish during the strides?

What do your arms do? Do they help?

Which part of your body leads the movement?

Can you run with other parts leading?

(b) Show the difference in the way you use your feet during slow and fast running.

Can you start slowly and finish quickly?

Show sudden and slow changes in speed.

(c) How do you use your body when you run vigorously? Run lightly?

(d) Run all over the gymnasium floor so that you never bump into anyone.

Can you run so that you are always in a space away from everyone else?

Can you run straight across the floor without changing direction?

Show the difference between straight, curved, and twisted running patterns.

Into which other directions can you run?

(e) Can you show a sequence of running which shows changes in

speed and direction while using different parts of your feet?
Run with sudden changes of direction and speed.
See how your shape changes as you run in different directions
with different parts leading.
How does your running change if you do not bend your
knees?
What happens to your running if one side of the body is
more important than the other?
Can you find a varied phrase of running which repeats
itself?
Copy the running sequence shown by another.
Develop a sequence with a partner.
Develop a matching sequence; a contrasting sequence.

BRIDGING

(a) Show me bridges over a line, mat, or rope.
Are there other parts on which you can support your
bridge?
Can you change to other parts while retaining your bridge?
Can you move one end of your bridge while the other end
is still?
Can you change your bridge from one part to another?
Do you need to use both ends of your body?
Can you use one side of the top half and the other side of the
bottom half?

(b) Can you change the supports slowly, quickly?
Show a change of supporting parts which starts quickly and
finishes slowly.
Show a sequence of sudden and slow changes.

(c) Show me several bridges which span varying distances.
Show high bridges with different bases; wide bridges with
different bases.
Can you make curved, twisted, bent bridges?
Can you change from one type to the other while keeping
one end still?
Can you transfer one end to another place?

(d) Make a bridge with a partner, then over and under a partner. Link together three bridges which show differences in base of support and shape.

Work out a sequence with your partner in which you both make the same use of direction, but show a contrast in the use of time.

NATURAL ACTIVITIES

In gymnastics the learning is based on the natural activities of walking, running, hopping, jumping, landing, balancing, rolling, somersaulting, wheeling, climbing, hanging, and swinging. The gross motor skills experienced at primary school level develop largely as a result of maturation and environmental experience. The finer body control which can result from the use of gymnastic apparatus in the secondary school is more dependent on directed discovery and consolidation through guidance but the teaching is still based on the utilization of the natural activities. The child's previous reactions to a similar but perhaps less problematical situation are reorganized and integrated with new learning to give a new pattern of response but not a new activity.

Progression in learning has three aspects:

1 *The range of activities experienced*, e.g. rolling, jumping, climbing. This is dependent on a balanced programme over a term; a simple matter of sound preparation and recording.
2 *The variations possible within one activity*. For example, jumping may involve stretched, tucked, or twisted movements of the body. The class may be asked to develop a simple movement and then given the opportunity to find variations of it. The initial problem is followed by suggestion and question. A child could practise an activity, perfect it to his own satisfaction, vary it, complicate it, add to it, and finish with a sequence of activities which he then needs to clarify. Children love to complicate physical activity. They learn a simple activity like skipping and then become absorbed in finding ways of making it more challenging. Basic skills are elaborated and combined,

often in very original ways, as the child demonstrates his proficiency and versatility. The change from authoritarian teaching to a discovery approach owes much of its impetus in physical education to the addition of 'variation' to the material. The teacher should lead the children into situations where they are able to use their natural inventiveness and imagination on gymnastic activity.

3 *The standard of performance.* To improve the quality of his performance the child must know how to practise in order to improve. To add refinement to an experimental beginning he should:

(a) through exploration have decided the basic form of the activity,

(b) be able to evalute his own ability and experience relative to the activity,

(c) repeat the activity so that he gains insight into the problems posed by his body and the apparatus,

(d) become aware of, and able to clarify, the movement factors involved.

The teacher should be able to help by drawing the attention of the class to selected performances and emphasizing the way in which the body is being used to answer the problems. This should assist them in developing the ability to criticize their own performance and to appreciate the work of others.

I have attempted to explain the way in which a progressive approach to education may be applied to the presentation of gymnastics. An analysis of teaching into this approach or that approach is a useful theoretical exercise as it clarifies the educational objectives. I have used it as a means of explanation by contrast; one can gain greater understanding of progressive methods by comparing them with formal methods. However, I must emphasize that most teachers will use a selected mixture of approaches over a long period and will bias the presentation one way or another as the situation demands.

A democratic approach to teaching is not easy for the

teacher. It demands constant thought and attention, flexibility and originality, patience and belief, and may be outside the capacity of some teachers. When the teacher has been conditioned to formal methods during his own secondary education he may find the principles difficult to accept. When many of his colleagues are using formal methods and the children have been conditioned to a more passive attitude to learning he may find the method difficult to present. But, persevere, for although demanding and time consuming it is the only way of teaching which guarantees a positive attitude towards the subject in the senior classes. Teacher–pupil cooperation, peer stimulus, and group approval are possibly the strongest motivating forces during the years thirteen to sixteen; the presentation suggested in the succeeding chapters makes extensive use of these factors in learning in the gymnasium.

CHAPTER TWO

Activity Development

The first task for the teacher is to define the purpose of his gymnastic scheme of work. Objectives are based on personal beliefs and therefore vary but tend now to be based on the 'accumulation of experience' rather than the 'accomplishment of objectives'. These experiences are of a physical nature involving skilful use of the body in as many situations as the gymnastic facilities will allow; of an intellectual nature involving the understanding and appreciation of gymnastic movement; and of a social nature involving partner and group work and the development of attitudes towards work, the group, and the teacher.

Initial interest and achievement are necessary if the scheme of work is to be developed successfully and it is important that the work of the secondary school should follow the work of the primary school as naturally as possible. The children should have the opportunity to repeat familiar activities and become more at ease with activities which they have experienced in a limited way. The first lessons give the opportunity for the practice of fundamental activities in the new environment of the gymnasium. Past experiences are reinforced and extended and new experiences are added. It is thought preferable to 'generalize' the initial activity experience rather than develop separate activities in any detail. The boy runs, jumps, and rolls; or, climbs, hangs, swings, and lands in a sequence of movements and is not asked to consider how he does it or how the activities may be varied. 'Look, I can do this,' is the first objective. This section may be termed the renewal of activity experience and the development of body management. For example:

Lesson One

FLOOR WORK
Running, walking, and stepping

APPARATUS
Mounting
Stepping or hanging and climbing
Jumping, sliding, or swinging off

Lesson Two

FLOOR WORK
Skipping, hopping, and stopping

APPARATUS
Jumping on
Moving along the apparatus
Getting off using feet and hands

Lesson Three

FLOOR WORK
Stepping and balancing

APPARATUS
Getting on using the hands
Balancing on the apparatus
Jumping or swinging or heaving off

Lesson Four

FLOOR WORK
Dodging, creeping, and sliding

APPARATUS
Jumping on
Performing an activity on the apparatus
Sliding off
Finishing with a balance away from the apparatus

17

Lesson Five

FLOOR WORK
Wheeling and rolling

APPARATUS
Use the hands to get on
Moving across and getting off
Finishing with a roll
Adding movement from feet to hands to feet

Lesson Six

FLOOR WORK
Jumping, falling, and crawling

APPARATUS
Activities which show lowering, rising, and turning
Movements of the body

Lesson Seven

FLOOR WORK
Bridging and balancing

APPARATUS
Bridging from floor to apparatus
On the apparatus
From apparatus to floor
Showing a bridging sequence

Lesson Eight

FLOOR WORK
Jumping and landing

APPARATUS
Showing a sequence of four activities which includes a jump and
a roll

The floor work should be performed on the *floor* and at first should not include small apparatus. Mats, hoops, and benches, although an essential part of the work are a hindrance in these initial lessons. They provide an obstacle to a natural rhythm and flow of movement and take attention away from the body. As long as the rolling and falling activities commence near to the floor there will be no discomfort and the patterns of movement will be unlimited.

The apparatus work will have a greater demand on weight management and the time allotted should allow exploration and discovery and sufficient consolidation. It should take up half to two-thirds of the lesson.

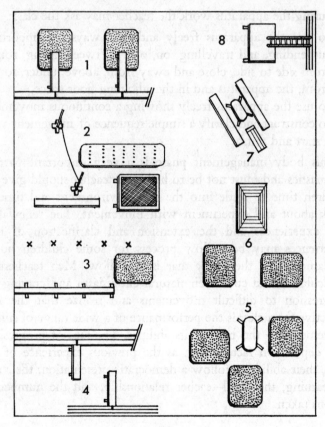

GROUP APPARATUS FOR THESE LESSONS

1 Beam at hanging height. Two sloping benches fixed on beam with lower ends on mats.
2 Agility mat and trampette, bench, jumping stands and rope at knee height.
3 Climbing ropes linked with wall bars and mat.
4 Double beams at chest and stretch height; linked by benches to window ladder.
5 Horse with mats on three sides.
6 Box four sections, and two mats away from box.
7 Buck, spring-board, and two benches.
8 A large table and a short strong ladder to wall bars.

During the apparatus work the teacher may ask the class:

1 to use the apparatus freely and find ways of supporting, suspending, and travelling, on, over, between, along, round, from side to side, close and away from, above, under, to and from, the apparatus and in the adjoining floor space,
2 to use the apparatus freely showing a continuous movement,
3 to construct and clarify a simple sequence of movement with a start and finish.

This body management phase is a very important part of gymnastics and must not be rushed. The teacher should give the children time to settle into the new environment and time to think about and experiment with movement. The renewal of past experiences and the extension and clarification of new experiences may be a slow process for some children but is fundamental to the work that is to follow. Men teachers in particular should curb their natural enthusiasm and craving for progression to difficult movements and realize that the first objective for a class is the performance of a wide range of simple movements to the best of its abilities. The rate of progression will depend on factors such as the previous experience of the class, their ability to follow a democratic presentation, their rate of learning, the pupil–teacher relationship, and the number of lessons taken.

CHAPTER THREE

Quantitative Development of Gymnastic Activity

Having provided the opportunity for practising, re-examining, and extending the natural activities in a new environment, the second phase of teaching emerges gradually. This phase may be termed 'clarification'. This is a process during which the child develops an awareness of the ways in which the body may be used. The emphasis of the teaching swings from management of the whole body in such a way that an activity is performed somehow, to an elementary understanding of the 'functional relationship' of the parts of the body during movement. For example the teacher may ask the class:

1 to get on, and jump or swing off—stressing the action of one part of the body,
2 to get on using one part of the body, and off using another. Specify the use of one part; e.g.

1 leave with weight on the hands, move on to the apparatus with feet together, show a movement which incorporates a leg swing;
2 use different parts of the body to receive and transfer weight along the apparatus,
3 move off the apparatus and absorb weight and momentum by using the legs. Can you absorb weight by using other parts of the body?

4 find ways of controlling and stopping the body after movement;

5 lead movements on to, along, and off the apparatus with different parts of the body.

The performer is encouraged to become aware of the movement of his whole body and conscious of the way in which parts of his body are working. The action of one part may become stressed while the scope of movement of another part becomes diminished and refined, giving a clearer pattern to the activity. He becomes conscious of the movements required to perform activities such as jumping, climbing, balancing, rolling, bridging.

THEME LESSONS

Having reached the stage where the children have extended their range and experience of activities and have developed some conscious awareness of the action of the parts of the body during movement, the teacher may introduce 'theme' lessons rather than 'activity' lessons. A theme lesson takes one aspect of movement and develops it throughout the lesson; it makes use of varied and unspecified activities in order to extend one movement experience. For example, the activities of balancing, transferring, bridging, rolling, and wheeling may be used to widen and clarify the experience of taking weight on large and small surfaces of the body. The problem of which activity to select in answer to the task is left to the child. Theme lessons are likely to be more successful if they emerge from a sound base of activity experience. The children then have a reasonable movement vocabulary to call upon to help solve the rather more difficult problems set by a theme.

A theme lesson gives complete linkage between the task set for the floor work and the apparatus work which follows. By the end of the floor work the class have practised a way of moving which can be transferred and adapted to each group of apparatus in turn, although the activities used may be different. One task imposes a general limitation which is common to all activities being developed on the apparatus. This makes the initial explanation simple even though the group teaching may be more difficult for the young teacher.

The first group of theme lessons used is usually concerned with *weight transference*. Tasks are given relating to parts of the body and involving movements in which the weight is taken by feet, knees, hips, front, back, chest, shoulders, head, or by two or more parts. The tasks may first be attempted in a fairly confined floor space and after practice and some success, a similar task is attempted involving travelling movements. For example, lessons may be developed from:

1   the use of the feet in movements about the gymnasium and on the apparatus, and the transfer of weight to other parts of the body,
2   taking weight on large and small surfaces,
3   initiating movement and absorbing weight,
4   lifting and lowering the body weight,
5   suspending, swinging, and rotating the body,
6   stable, unstable, and travelling movement.

After problems of weight transference have been worked out, and practised on the floor, the teacher may wish to introduce ropes, hoops, bean-bags, benches, and mats as intermediate steps between the floor work and the large apparatus. Boys in particular seem to enjoy the objective use of small apparatus in this way; it helps to introduce the more difficult problems of the relationship between the body and the large apparatus.

The second group of theme lessons is concerned with body *shape and function*. It is perhaps unrealistic to separate lessons on weight transference from lessons incorporating tasks based on shape. The majority of teachers would have stressed 'body shape' during the very early lessons. However, it is suggested here that theme lessons on shape are a later development although the shape of the body may already have received emphasis in an attempt to improve quality of performance.

This group of lessons is concerned with dynamic shape and not static shape. It is the 'function' of stretching, curling, and twisting that is required and should be thought of as activity involving travelling movements rather than a quality to be demonstrated. Examples of the kind of work that may be included are:

1 Use the apparatus and show stretched shapes.
2 Show a stretched and curled shape.
3 Show a twisting movement on, over, under, or off the apparatus.
4 Attempt a sequence of movement which shows changes in the shape of the body.
5 Show how a stretch on the floor can lead into a curl on the apparatus.

The quantitative aspect of gymnastic experience may be developed through activity lessons which lead to theme lessons as the understanding of the class increases. The content of each lesson presented is somewhat narrower in experience than the 'body management' phase of the scheme of work. A lesson would probably be based on one or more of the movement experiences of:

1 *Locomotion*
Step and carriage; walking, running, striding, checking, arresting, stopping.

2 *Transfers*
Selected use of parts of the body to produce unorthodox travelling, e.g. crawling, bridging, sliding.

3 *Jumping and Springing*
Giving and receiving impetus. Variation in jumping and landing.

4 *Rotation*
Rotation around different axes to give rolls, somersaults and wheeling activities.

5 *Balance*
Supports below the body; maintaining and losing equilibrium.

6 *Suspending*
Supports above the body by hooking 'body-parts' on to the apparatus. Movements to include hanging, heaving, traversing, climbing, and swinging.

One of the main objectives of these lessons is to draw attention to the function of the body during movement and the teacher would emphasize:

1 the part of the body taking weight,
2 how the 'body-parts' cooperate with each other to give travelling movements; the parts giving and receiving impetus,
3 the use of the hands and the trunk in travelling,
4 parts needing stressed action in order to complete and improve an activity; parts moving and parts still,
5 leading activities with different parts of the body,
6 using parts to control and stop travelling activities,
7 parts on which the body can balance,
8 parts which can absorb momentum,
9 parts coming close together, or going far apart,
11 bending: around varied centres, in different directions,
12 stretching: exploring zones of movement: pin, leaf, and spiky shapes,
13 twisting: regions of the body used in twisting movements; incorporating twisting movements into activities,
14 symmetry: use of one and both sides of the body.

EXAMPLES OF LESSONS

Lesson One—Jumping

INTRODUCTORY ACTIVITY
Activities with a rope; show changes in your body shape.

Running
Show a pattern of running, the use of feet and knees, with ropes on floor. Put ropes away, and run with varied use of direction. Note lightness and control are important.

FLOOR WORK

To improve the take-off in jumping.

1 Practise a standing jump.
2 Practise and show effort in take-off and control in landing.
3 As above, after taking two steps.
4 Show different use of the feet. Select a double take-off jump and use the demonstration to teach technique.
5 Show a jump from two feet. Use questioning to give an understanding of variety in take-off, i.e. single foot, two feet, effort, speed and length of approach run.

APPARATUS

The group apparatus to be selected so that jumping on to, off, or over a piece of apparatus is possible.

TASK

Link a jump with two different activities, e.g.
jump, roll and balance;
swing, jump and bridge;
heave, balance and jump.

Lesson Two—Jumping

INTRODUCTORY ACTIVITY

Practice jumps with a partner, over a partner, on to partner's back, or into his arms.
How does the take-off effect the flight?

FLOOR WORK

Jumping with emphasis on shape:

1 Jump with a stretch.
2 Use a different stretch; improve it.
3 Jump with a different shape.
4 Jump and make yourself as small as possible.
5 Jump and touch your feet. How many different ways can you do this?

6 Jump and bend your hips; with knees bent; knees straight.
7 How can you vary your body shape?

CLASS ACTIVITY
Benches—in small groups.
1 Show a sequence of two jumps with contrasting shape, with similar shape.
2 Show a change of direction in the sequence.
3 Vary jumps over and off the bench showing rebounding, rolling, or transferring as preparation for the next jump. Build up a sequence which includes three jumps and a change of direction.

Lesson Three—Jumping

INTRODUCTORY ACTIVITY
Run and jump with an immediate rebound into a new direction. After landing show a stretched balance on one foot.

Running
Shadowing a partner from the rear. (Exact repetition of speed, stride, knee action demanded from shadower. It is not a chasing game.)

CLASS ACTIVITY
Benches and box-tops; groups of three or four.
1 Group cooperation to produce jumping sequences with continuous use of the bench.
2 The group sequence adapted to show varied take-off; contrasting body shape in flight, and a balanced landing.

Lesson Four—Jumping

INTRODUCTORY ACTIVITY
Bridging and jumping chase: half the class make a bridge, the remainder jump two and then make a bridge. Bridges change over when jumped twice.

FLOOR WORK

1 Recall a known sequence.
2 Demonstrate continuity and varied use of the body in the sequences.
3 Observe and copy partner's shape.
4 With a partner synchronize four jumps which have varied shapes and directional changes.

APPARATUS WORK

Group	Task
1 Ropes, bench, four hoops.	Swing to balanced landing on bench; backward swing off, landing with change of direction; finish with a jump from a hoop. Vary by starting on the bench. Group to practise synchronized swings and jumps in pairs or threes.
2 Beam (in 10), two sloping benches.	A circuit of balance travels finishing with a jump.
3 Beam (in 17), jumping stands and rope.	Swinging heave over rope. Add change of direction. Return over ends of beam.
4 Window ladder and two benches.	Jumps from bench to varied landings using feet, or feet and hands. Return, jumping over bench.
5 Horse	Free practice of activities, moving over, under, and on to apparatus.
6 Agility mat, buck, trampette.	Pairs; sequence of two jumps using the apparatus, one with partner assistance.
7 Box three sections, and springboard.	Distance jumps to land in controlled balance on box top. Dismount into a roll and return jump on to box. Dismount and show an activity on the hands. (Should be two on the box at once.)
8 Rolled mattress and mat.	Roll over the mattress and change direction on landing. Move into a jump on and off wall bars.

APPARATUS PLAN

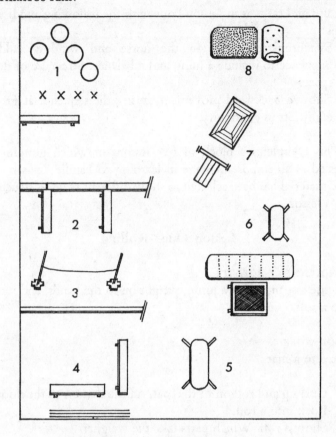

Lesson Five—Jumping

INTRODUCTORY ACTIVITY

In threes. Jumping activities from two feet over and between partners, showing stretched and tucked body shape.

FLOOR WORK

Small groups using benches sloped to wall bars, vaulting apparatus and springboards, etc. Jumps off and over the apparatus with assistance from the group or a partner. Emphasis on assisted flight.

APPARATUS

Groups and tasks as in Lesson Four with the following modifications:

(*a*) Synchronized work on the horse and window ladder. Sequence to include a jump and a balance. Stress use of floor space.

(*b*) Show a backward movement during the sequence at group eight. Stress continuity.

This completes a block of five lessons in which jumping is stressed as an important stage in learning to handle one's body. The material has been selected to show different ways of structuring a lesson.

Lesson One—Rolling

INTRODUCTORY ACTIVITY

Practise a sequence of a jump, weight on to the hands, and move into a roll.

FLOOR WORK

Three to a mat.

1 Curl up and roll on to the mat, off the mat on to the floor.
2 Rock into a roll.
3 Show a roll. Which parts take the weight?
4 Roll using the trunk only.
5 Roll across different parts of the back.
6 Roll from different starting positions.
7 Roll and finish on different parts of the body.
8 Roll and try to keep your legs straight, your arms straight.
9 Roll with feet high, with feet low, with feet astride.
10 Stretch into a roll, turn into a roll, twist into a roll.
11 Jump and roll, roll into a jump.
12 Show a sequence of two different rolls and clarify the use of the parts of the body.

APPARATUS

The apparatus plan could be the same as for the last lesson, omitting 5, with the following modifications:

1 Replace hoops with mats (individual type if available).
2 Place mats under the lower ends of the benches.
3 Place a mat on the far side of the rope. Second beam at waist height.
4 and 5 These two groups to combine, add a bench between horse and nearest bench.
6 Remove buck and add mat.
7 Add buck at right angles to box.
8 Add one mat to each side.

TASK

Practise a sequence of activities which involve rolling and rotary movements.

Lesson Two—Rolling

INTRODUCTORY ACTIVITY

All fours, dodge and mark with no turning allowed, i.e. head always facing the same direction.

FLOOR WORK

Rolling on the floor, or on large thin sheets of rubber or carpet underlay.

1 Repeat a rolling sequence from Lesson One.
2 Place the accent on shape by introducing bending, twisting, and stretching.
3 Show a rolling pattern composed of rolls with,
   (a) the body straight,   (c) the body rolled up,
   (b) the body folded,   (d) the body twisted.
4 Attempt a roll which starts with one shape and changes to another.
5 Find a sequence of two rolls which show all four shapes.

31

APPARATUS
Plan as in Lesson One on rolling.

TASK
Show a continuous sequence of activity making maximum use of the group apparatus and demonstrate:

1 changing shape of the body,
2 a sliding activity with head down or hand-standing into a roll.
Finish the sequence with a roll on the floor.

Lesson Three—Rolling

INTRODUCTORY ACTIVITY
Rolling dodge ball.
Two boys with a football at each end of the gym. Class scattered over the floor in sitting position. Balls to be rolled from end to end. Boys dodge by rolling. When hit they should make a three-point bridge and if they can get the ball through the bridge they may join in again. The object is to score as many hits as possible in a given time. Ball should be rolled at moderate speed.

APPARATUS
Plan as last lesson.

TASKS
1 Swing over the bench into a roll; swing backwards off the bench into a roll. Link the two activities into a continuous sequence.
2 Use the apparatus to show rolling activities up and down the bench and from bench to floor.
3 Circling activities on the beams linked with rolling under and over the rope.
4 and 5 With a partner produce a combined sequence which includes at least one jump, balance, hang and bridge.
Show good use of the floor space.

6 Jumping and rolling activities which include turning movements.
7 Jumping with assisted flight.
8 Experiment with fast-rolling activities.

The three rolling lessons give apparatus tasks for each lesson although one would obviously not attempt a full circuit in any one lesson. There is enough material in each of these for a follow-up lesson with more opportunity for practice and more emphasis on the parts of the body, floor patterns, and partner work.

Lesson One—Balance

INTRODUCTORY ACTIVITY
Practise running and walking, and on a signal hold a balanced position on one foot, or foot and hands, keeping as high as possible.

FLOOR WORK
1 Show a balanced position on a large area of the body. Are there other large surfaces on which you can take weight?
2 Balance on a small area. Find other small parts on which you can take weight.
3 Balance on an immovable surface of the body. How many can you find?
4 Balance on a movable part of the body. How many can you find?
5 Balance on two movable parts, on three, and on one surface and one jointed part, a surface and two jointed parts.
6 Transfer weight from a surface to two jointed parts and balance.
7 Show a stretched balance, a curled balance.
8 Walk into a balance. Jump into a balance.
   Roll into a balance. Run, stop, and balance.
   Twist, fall, and balance.

APPARATUS
1 Ropes, bench supported between buck and wall bars.
2 Beam high, trampette, two mats, and a bench.
3 Ropes supporting a swinging bench, two sloping benches rib uppermost to wall bars.
4 Window ladder and agility mattress.
5 Horse and two benches.
6 Agility mattress.
7 Box (three sections), two benches.
8 Mats.

APPARATUS PLAN

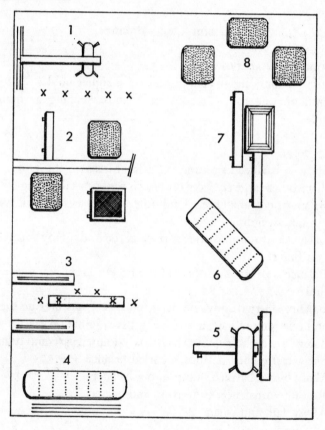

TASK

Use the apparatus to find out:

(a) What parts can take weight while the body is still?
(b) What parts can support while the body is moving?

Lesson Two—Balance

INTRODUCTORY ACTIVITY

Show a matching sequence with a partner in which the body transfers from a stretched balance to a curled balance.

FLOOR WORK

1 Practise balanced positions in which some or all of your weight is on hands, feet, elbows, or knees.
2 Show a balance. Change the shape without losing balance.
3 Show a balance in which the body is twisted.
4 Balance with the feet highest.
5 Cooperate with a partner in balancing.
6 Balance with a partner taking some weight, and then all of your weight.
7 Pairs. Tripod balances mirroring partner's movements.
8 Interlocking balances with partner.

APPARATUS

Plan as last lesson.

GROUP TASKS

1 Rope swing to bench or buck. Jump off and roll into a balance.
2 Bounce from trampette to hang on beam. Swing to land and balance. Follow with a jumping and rolling sequence.
3 Sitting, kneeling, and standing balances on the swinging bench. Link with an activity on each bench and on wall bars.
4 Trunk balances on window ladder and angular balances on agility mat. Group cooperate to show changing patterns.
5 'Pyramids' on horse and bench. Experimental group balances.
6 Timed sequences with partner, showing extensive use of floor space.

7 Jump on to box top and balance; melt into a roll off and on to the bench; bridge between bench and floor; move into a wheel or hand-walking activity.
8 Pairs. Free activity supporting partner in stillness and in action.

Balancing can be included as an interesting ingredient of the majority of sequences on the apparatus. Complete lessons on balancing should not be overstressed.

Lesson One—Transferring Weight

INTRODUCTORY ACTIVITY
Use hands and feet alternately to escape hopping chasers.

FLOOR WORK
1 Show movements in which the weight goes on to and off the hands.
2 Above with stretched and curled positions.
3 Weight alternately on hands and feet.
4 Weight on hands, feet still, and move hands in different directions.
5 Keep hands still and move feet. How many different ways of moving the feet can you find (walking, jumping, swinging, single and double take-off)? Show different leg actions (knees bent and straight, apart, together, one leg leading).
6 Hands still, can you place the hips in different positions? Hips above hands; which leg provides the force? Stress this action. What is the shape of your back?
7 Weight transferred from feet to hands to another part.
8 Weight from feet to hands and into a bridge; into different bridges.

APPARATUS
Plan as for lesson on balance.

TASK

Use the hands so that they are the first part of the body to arrive on the apparatus and the last part to leave.

Lesson Two—Transfers based on Wheeling and Bridging

INTRODUCTORY ACTIVITY

Cartwheels.

FLOOR WORK

1 Weight from feet to hands to feet with different use of legs.
2 Practise wheeling and walking activities on the hands.
3 Stretch on the hands and into a bridge. Bridge on different parts. In different directions.
4 Bridge facing the floor and move smoothly into a bridge facing the ceiling.
5 Bridge on movable parts, on immovable parts, and on both.
6 Bridge with a partner and show contrasting shapes.
7 Practise a sequence of cartwheel, handstand and bridge. Change the order.

APPARATUS

Experiment with activities in which weight is taken by the hands,
(a) head below hands,
(b) head above hands.

Lesson Three—Transfers

INTRODUCTORY ACTIVITY

Running patterns with a partner leading with different parts of the body.

FLOOR WORK

1 Practise transfers from hands to other parts of the body.
2 Transfers from other parts of the body to the feet.

3 Link activities which move into varying directions through using the above ideas.

Emphasize floor pattern, parts of body, shape, stretching, curling, folding, and twisting, to improve individual sequences.

APPARATUS

Transfer during known activities. Clarify the use of changing parts and give attention to smooth and jerky transfers, and slow and quick transfers.

Practise activities which do not start and finish on the same part.

CHAPTER FOUR

Qualitative Development of Gymnastic Activity

Having revised and extended the movement experience of the class, the next step is to widen understanding of the *action* of moving. Attention is now directed not only to the parts of the body involved but to 'how' and 'where' the body moves. The teaching is now concerned with the clarification of body-awareness by thoughtful and conscious use of the *Factors of motion* present in all movement.

Although the accomplishment of an activity is still the basis of the work the thoughts of the performer are concentrated on the 'feel' and the path of movement of the performance. The accomplishment is no longer sufficient; the teacher's task is to encourage *quality* of performance. Quality is demonstrated by a performer through the selection of the appropriate factors. He attempts to display what he feels is the correct degree of force, amount of time, quantity of space, line of direction, and type of shape, and to give his interpretation of the rhythm, and flow of movement involved in the activity. He becomes aware of the factors present and grades them consciously during the performance. An understanding of the factors present and the ability to demonstrate their presence is helped by questions along the lines suggested below.

1 *'Body-parts'*
   Which parts take weight? Which parts move?
   Which parts receive stress? Which parts are still?

2 *Quick and Slow*
Can you vary the speed of the movement; of phases of the movement; of the parts of the body involved?

3 *Weight*
How much force must be included to complete the movement successfully? Does the movement demand varying degrees of force? Is there a rhythm to the movement which combines force and time?

4 *Space*
How is space used during the activity? How much space is taken up by your body and by the whole activity? In which direction are you moving? At what levels does movement take place? Into which zones do the 'body-parts' move?

Student-teachers find this phase of the scheme difficult to develop and an attempt to explain the relation of the motion factors to gymnastic teaching may be helpful. The accepted analysis pioneered in gymnastics by women teachers includes the factors of time, space, weight, and flow.

SPACE
Observation of movement will show that the body moves through a certain quantity of space. By different use of the parts of the body the activity can vary in the amount of space used. The attention of the class may be drawn to the use of:

(a) *Personal Space*
The parts of the body may be moved through various positions so that maximum to minimum space is used. Experimentation will show that in order to vary the space used the body will stretch, curl, or twist.

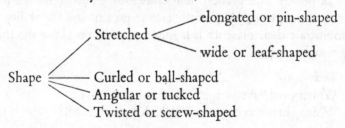

Stretched — elongated or pin-shaped
Stretched — wide or leaf-shaped
Shape — Curled or ball-shaped
Shape — Angular or tucked
Shape — Twisted or screw-shaped

These basic shapes may be symmetrical or asymmetrical, and will be combined and changed during the flux of movement in order to accomplish the activity.

(b) *General Space*
The activity moves through a maximum to minimum quantity of space according to the distance covered, the height attained, and the shape of the body.

(c) *Direction*
The direction of movement in relation to the body may be forwards, sideways, backwards, upwards, or downwards or a combination of these.

WEIGHT

Weight is a word which men do not like to use to describe this motion factor as they think of weight in terms of its usual scientific meaning. Force or power, an intensity factor, is a term generally preferred.

The use of muscular force becomes evident when tasks relating to stressed action of a 'body-part' are given, e.g. the leg drive in rolling; powerful use of the arms in jumping, the heaving action of the arms in climbing; a vigorous leg swing in wheeling on to the hands.

The force demanded and the time factor are closely tied in the performance of gymnastic movement. The force exerted depends on the speed desired and on the use of space. Men teachers have tended to approach the use of force from a time and space limitation, e.g. a high jump, a roll with flight, a fast leg swing. An awareness of force and firmness is achieved to a great extent by the feel of muscular contraction and relaxation involved in:

1 the initial trial, error, and success of activity performances in which the feeling of forceful action is gradually clarified and remembered,

2 the experimental performance of time and space problems applied to the activity.

This awareness of 'energy output' should not only be related to the peak force involved in completion of the whole activity. It should include an appreciation of the rhythm of strong and light muscle action which blends into the movement continuity of the activity. It is the ability to vary, adjust, and clarify the force exerted which gives smooth and skilful performance and good body control. There is therefore a place in gymnastics for lightness and relaxation as well as forceful action, and attention may be drawn to activities which use contrasting qualities of force in an attempt to widen experience and understanding. The conscious use of force in an economical and skilful way, is essential to gymnastic performance and is dependent on this wide experience of both strong and light movement.

TIME

The majority of activities performed on gymnastic apparatus have an optimum speed; the speed at which an individual can perform the activity successfully and safely. A complete activity is from starting position to finishing position and involves a preparatory or approach phase, the executive or action phase, and the recovery phase. Initial experiments enable the performer to discover the appropriate speed for the whole activity, the 'natural time' for the performance by that person.

At first children tend to perform naturally, even instinctively, with little conscious awareness of how the time factor is being used. They will, for example, perform a rolling activity in which the approach, the take-off, the roll, and the recovery movements are all at the same speed. This speed will vary from one child to the next according to their movement characteristics, but the individual tends to perform the activity at the same speed on every performance. By the time the qualitative stage has been reached body awareness and control should be sufficiently advanced to enable the class to experiment with varying use of time. They should first show contrasting use of time between different activities, and then attempts may be made to do the same activity at varying speeds. Six alternatives are possible:

	Preparation Time	Executive Time	Recovery Time	Duration Time
1	Fast	Fast	Fast	Minimum
2	Slow	Fast	Fast	Medium fast
3	Fast	Fast	Slow	Medium fast
4	Slow	Slow	Fast	Medium slow
5	Fast	Slow	Slow	Medium slow
6	Slow	Slow	Slow	Maximum

It is expected that one of these permutations will be natural to the performer and the others will be rather more difficult or even impossible. Even if he finds the task impossible he will have benefited from the experience and will be more aware of the nature of time in movement.

The table illustrates that there are two aspects of time: speed of movement, and duration of activity. One activity may include very speedy movements but may be of long duration, whilst a different activity may be of short duration, yet includes slow movements.

It is in *sequence work* that the time factor really comes to the fore. When a number of movements have been linked together successfully, the performer may then demonstrate his grasp of time awareness by showing contrasting qualities of fast and sustained movements. Slowness may be demonstrated in a sequence by including rolling movements, recovery movements, and stable linking movements, and may be contrasted with the fast explosive movements in jumping and springing. The stillness of balance extends experience still further and enhances the appeal of the sequence both to the performer and observer.

Through experience of fast and sustained movement the class will develop understanding of the time factor. It is at this stage, when the child feels that he has the power to control movement sufficiently to demonstrate clearly the degree of speed or sustainment he wishes to present, that gymnastic activity takes on a richness and becomes a form of physical expression that can give immense satisfaction.

43

FLOW

The body, according to its size, shape, strength, and mobility, has a natural flow of movement which is peculiar to the individual. This characteristic will be seen in all his movements, running, playing, etc., as well as being a recognized part of his gymnastic movement. Every boy has a sense of muscle rhythm which is observable. If this flow of muscle action is trainable it would appear to be so only in a strict environmental sense, i.e. any natural rhythm of action becomes adapted and absorbed into a skilled activity that is specific to a certain situation.

A flow of movement in gymnastics would appear to be the same as body control, yet flowing and controlling are opposing terms. 'Bound flow', used to describe the type of control which the preciseness of gymnastics seeks, is not a term one wishes to apply to gymnastic movement. Controlling muscle action to give a skilful performance may be a better way of approaching what is needed in the body. The environment and the activity dictate the flow of action through the body. When looked at from this point of view, flow becomes 'function of the parts of the body', and not a separate factor. An analysis of the gymnastic situation divides flow into:

(a) the control of the body,
(b) the continuity of the activity.

The continuity or fluency of the activity as a whole is dependent on the use of time and space and once again does not bring an additional factor into play. In seeking fluency in a single activity or in sequence work, the boy's task is to maintain the flow of movement through the body or through space so that the sensation of continuity is experienced.

The word 'flow' describing the amount of liberty or restraint placed on body action is more applicable to dance, and continuity is perhaps the word which describes what is needed in gymnastics. Continuity is a descriptive word and is displayed in varying ways rather than used.

Lessons Extending Quality of Movement

The motion factors provide an analysis of movement from which the qualitative phase of the gymnastic scheme may be developed. They are the means by which the teacher is able to direct thought and action towards a higher standard of performance. Tasks are set which give the class an opportunity for experimentation on the use of the motion factors, the objective being an awareness of their presence in movement and the ability to display their use during the performance of known activities. The lessons would emphasize:

1 that the arms, legs, and trunk may be used to supply and receive impetus and to receive, support, and transfer body weight,

2 that body shape may be varied,

3 that the path of movement may be forwards, backwards, sideways, upwards, downwards, or a combination of these in a direct or flexible way,

4 that movement may take place at high and low levels on the floor and apparatus,

5 that control of light and strong movement is necessary for the accurate accomplishment of skilled activity,

6 that an action may be graded between fast and slow, and the use of time may be changed during an activity,

7 that activities may be combined to give a movement sequence and continuity may be displayed by phrasing the flow of movement in particular ways.

The presentation of these lessons is difficult to give in written form and examples are of doubtful value. However a few selected lessons are tabulated, not for teaching purposes, but to provide material for illustration and for discussion.

Lesson—Jumping

INTRODUCTORY ACTIVITY

Benches out, a running pattern showing changes of speed and direction.

FLOOR WORK

1 Two jumps, one over bench.
2 Show a change of direction in second jump. Improve control and continuity.
3 Jump off the bench in different directions. With different body shapes.
4 Jump backwards off the bench, over the bench. Control landing.
5 Experiment with landing positions after a forward, sideways, or backward jump.
6 Vary the use of force—light and strong, upwards and forwards. Link this with use of direction.
7 Jump and turn. How far can you turn? Lead with head only. Use head and arms to turn. Control landing after a turn.
8 Show a sequence for three jumps to demonstrate varied use of space, direction and force.

APPARATUS

A sequence of a jump and two other activities which show changes in the use of space.

Lesson—Rolling

INTRODUCTORY ACTIVITY

Rolling position. Two chasers. When touched, boy must complete a roll without the part tagged touching the ground. Count numbers on floor after twenty seconds.

FLOOR WORK

1 Practise rolling in different directions.
2 Can you change direction during the roll?

46

3 Roll into different directions from the same starting position.
4 Choose one roll. Can you vary the shape?
5 Roll with varied use of space.
6 Show a roll which you can do very slowly. Show a very fast roll. Link the two together.
7 Start a roll slowly and finish quickly; the opposite.
8 Show three rolls each with a different shape.
   Link them together and show different use of time.
9 How can a roll be varied?
   (a) Direction.   (b) Shape.
   (c) Time.   (d) Parts taking weight.
   (e) Take-off.   (f) Starting and finishing positions.

APPARATUS
A sequence of activities which finishes with a roll; which includes a roll.

Lesson—Transfers based on Hopping, Falling, and Bridging

INTRODUCTORY ACTIVITY
Activities in which you take your partner's weight.

FLOOR WORK
Hopping
1 Hop with changes of direction.
   Stress use of the free leg swing.
2 Quick and slow hopping.
3 Develop a hopping pattern showing varied use of direction and time.

Falling
1 Hop into a fall.
2 In what order are 'body-parts' used to receive weight?
3 Use in a different order.
4 Fall on to different body-parts.

5 Fall in different directions.
Flexible and direct falling.
Turn and twist into a fall.
6 Lose balance slowly, quickly and fall.

Bridging
1 Use different body-parts to form bridges.
2 Move into and out of bridges showing quick and sustained movement.

Sequence
Practise a sequence of hopping, falling, and bridging. Develop a sequence of the three activities demonstrating the use of time and space, and include linking movements where necessary.

Lesson—Jumping and Wheeling Sequences

INTRODUCTORY ACTIVITY
Leap frog with partner.
Add a movement on the hands.

FLOOR WORK
Jumping
1 Practise a jump.
2 Make another jump with a different shape.
3 Link the two.

Weight on Hands
1 In a curled position, show a sustained movement.
2 In a stretched position, show a fast and vigorous movement.
3 Link the two.

Sequence
1 One of the jumps linked with weight on hands in a curled position.
2 The other jump linked with weight on hands stretched.

3 Link the two sequences into one and demonstrate:
   (*a*) fast and sustained movement,
   (*b*) contrasting use of space,
   (*c*) an angular pathway of movement.
4 Pairs, one to perform and one to coach.
   How can you help him to improve the sequence?
   Clarify the use of the motion factors.
   Improve control, continuity, the starting and finishing positions.

APPARATUS

Develop a sequence of a jump and roll and weight on hands with head above or below point of support.

(*a*) Activities in any order.
(*b*) Consider the use of time and space so that you may demonstrate the sequence and then explain to the class what aspects of time and space you were attempting to display.

These activity lessons will be interspersed with theme lessons based on time, weight, and space. One more lesson is included as an illustration of the type of material to present to a competent class.

Lesson—The Theme 'Level'

INTRODUCTORY ACTIVITY

Demonstrate a sequence of known activities which shows movements close to the ground, above the ground, and in the air.

FLOOR WORK

Build a sequence with a partner which shows high transfers, medium level balances, and low rolls.

The teacher asks for a clear starting and finishing position, a varied floor pattern with changes of direction and level, accurate repetition of shapes of movement and body, varied use of speed to bring out contrasts and accents, the use of many parts of the body.

49

APPARATUS

Each group to demonstrate an understanding of *level* in their group practice.

Apparatus specified by the teacher and arranged by the group of boys.

1 Mat, bench, trampette, rope.
   Task—Demonstrate group cooperation in using the apparatus. Show continuity and action in all three levels.
2 Box, springboard, beam at any height, two medicine balls.
   Task—as group one.
3 Ropes, agility mattress, buck.
   Task—Transfers with a rotation, group cooperation, and some manual assistance.
4 Double beam, springboard, bench, two mats.
   Task—Individual sequence of jumps, balances, and hanging.
5 Horse, bench, trampette, and window ladder.
   Task—Directional changes and floor pattern.
6 Choice of remaining apparatus.
   Group production of activity sequence showing contrasting use of time.

Sequence Work

The recent trend in school gymnastics has been to move away from the performance of single activities and to encourage the linking of a number of activities to give a sequence.

One cannot expect a young child to produce expressive sequences; he can only link together simple ideas. He finds difficulty in developing an idea as this demands a wide vocabulary of movement. As activity experience is extended, and the ability of the child to express quality of movement becomes readily observable, so will the sequence work grow in maturity from the simple movement to the planned sequence.

1 The first attempts at sequence work will be the joining together of two activities. One activity is placed in a space adjacent to the other so that a little 'bonding' occurs between the two. This sequence is practised on the floor and on the apparatus, e.g. a jump and a roll.

2 The sequence is formed from variations of one activity, e.g. practise a jump, improve the quality, find a different way of jumping, link the two jumps into a sequence, improve the linkage, improve the start and finish.

3 The third type of sequence is based on the use of the parts of the body. Find a sequence of movement from feet, to hands, to back, to feet; or choose several parts of the body on which you can support weight and, using these parts, show a sequence moving smoothly from one position to the next.

4 A sequence based on body action, e.g. a stretch and a curl.

5 Sequences built up by the addition of activities, e.g. perform a jump, add a rolling movement and practise the sequence; show me a balance, now add the balance to the sequence.

The parts of a sequence should be linked and moulded together so that one is not merely joining activities but is constructing something which is a whole and is finally inseparable. Linking activities together should mean that one grows out of the other, so that A becomes part of B and B cannot be shown without A. They now belong together and are no longer the original activities. It is this moulding together of movements that gives opportunity for personal expression.

When the child is able to demonstrate a reasonable quality in his work he can attempt to construct a sequence which emphasizes selected points and maintains a train of thought throughout.

The gymnast must learn how to arrange movements for the full meaning to be understood; how to place them in the context where they will be effective and harmonious. The phraseology must include a skilful use of movement with a suitable beginning, an observable growth, and an established ending.

When the sequence task is given what reaction follows? This is the way an experienced child should be thinking during practice.

'I have been asked to construct a sequence of movement in which I take weight on my hands in three ways. I can choose from many different ways for I can crawl, roll, walk, bridge, wheel, and balance on my hands.'

'I must be clear in showing how I use my hands—that this is a wheeling activity, the second a roll, and the third a bridge.'

'How shall I add expression? I shall do the first quickly and stretched, for the second my body will move into and out of a curl and will show a change of direction, and the third will be a slow twisting movement. I shall place a stop at the end of the first part so that I may bring the fast movement under control and shall keep the continuity going with an arm movement; the second will end with a slight pause and I shall slowly twist into the final phase.'

'Now more practice is needed, the middle section needs repeating a few times. Faster here, slower there, a greater swing during the change of direction. Fluency is coming and the sequence is nearly complete and ready to demonstrate.'

This is perhaps an imaginative description of sequence construction, but it outlines the essential characteristics and is included to show that a sequence is more than A+B+C.

The following examples illustrate the type of tasks which may be presented:

1 A sequence of a jump with a stretch and a roll with a change of direction, moving into a twist on the floor, finishing with a balance taking part of the weight on the head.
2 Link three rolls showing different use of time and space.
3 Roll and jump in different ways showing a clear distinction between sudden and sustained movement.
4 A sequence of activities which show sudden and lengthy transitions.

5 Choose four activities which demonstrate the use of your body while varying the use of time, space, and weight.
6 Use the apparatus to show the qualities of curling, stretching, and twisting while varying the use of time.

Having completed a sequence task the child should be able to add this to his repertoire and repeat it on future occasions. As part of the work he learns to observe and criticize constructively, and to demonstrate, share, and communicate. Perhaps the most fascinating aspect of sequence work is found in group cooperation. Children love to produce timed and matching sequences with a partner or a group.

CHAPTER FIVE

A Summary and Suggestions for Recording the Lessons

In Chapter One it was said that the presentation of educational gymnastics contains a sensible degree of guidance. This implies that the planning of objectives and the setting of standards is dependent upon cooperation between teacher and class.

Under these circumstances is it possible to foresee the way in which a lesson will develop, and to plan ahead? The teacher must know within certain limits where the lesson is to take him and how this lesson fits into the complete scheme of work. With experience the teacher is able to pose his questions and suggestions so that the range of movement practised is widened or narrowed according to the objectives of the lesson, but nevertheless difficulties arise in the recording of lessons and in the presentation of a balanced programme. The activity record chart has been devised to help the teacher solve this problem.

The chart is divided into the three phases of gymnastic experience.

A ACTIVITY DEVELOPMENT

The list of activities shows the wide range of movement experience possible in a gymnasium. They form the basis from which individual development and interpretation of movement is possible.

Teachers and children have a tendency to rely upon a select group of activities, i.e. jumps, balances, rolls, bridges, and wheels, which are the better-known movements, and to ignore the remainder. By checking the list of activities the teacher is able to ensure that the experience of the boys is not limited to the traditional gymnastic activities but includes the complete range of natural activities.

B QUANTITATIVE FACTORS

Extension of experience stems from:

(a) new activities,
(b) using other parts of the body to perform an activity,
(c) changing the function of the parts of the body,
(d) changing the path of movement,
(e) changing the environment.

New activities

This aspect is covered mainly by the section on activity development. It is thought of as increased range of experience, and not as a development of variation. The teacher should have a clear understanding of whether he wishes task-interpretation to give a new or different activity, a variation of the same activity or a choice of either. Movement-understanding and increased vocabulary is developed mainly through variation.

Parts of the body

The child may vary an activity by using other parts of his body to perform the same activity, e.g. walking may use the whole leg or parts of it. The supporting part may be, for example, the foot, the knee, on one foot and one knee, the heel of one foot and the ball of the other. The teacher should not attempt to encourage the development of many variations during one lesson, but should return to the problem for further exploration at convenient times. The inventive mind of the child will find innumerable variations and he must have ample opportunity to experience and register them. Obviously more time may be spent on one variation than on another according to the interest shown and the value which is placed on the movement. The child should not be hurried away from a variation if it is still in the thought-provoking stage.

Function

The basic activity, or one of the derivations, may be explored through drawing the child's attention to the function of the body in movement. During an activity the limbs or trunk may stretch, become angular, curl, or twist. They may give impetus to the body, or transfer or receive weight. It is possible to experiment with changes of action and stress, e.g. use of the arms in rolling, which result in interesting variations without changing the basic character of the activity.

The function of the parts of the body will change during performance, seldom is an activity confined to using one aspect of function. Whereas one tends to think of an isolated movement as demonstrating a single function, an activity usually combines two or more. Whilst climbing or rolling, the same parts may in turn be involved in stretching, curling, and twisting. It may be possible to use these functions in a strict order, combine them, or change the order, and so give the activity a change of character.

Spatial form of the movement

1   *Direction*—The child may distinguish:

(*a*) a change of direction resulting from a turn and a change of front,

(*b*) a change of direction by variation in the use of the body while maintaining the same front.

The former is perhaps the natural method and the child will probably show a change of direction by incorporating a turn between activities. The teacher should ask for changes of direction in which turning is not part of the problem so that a variation in the form of the basic activity will evolve; for example, a change of direction during walking will involve different use of the feet and leading with a different part of the body, and in rolling, different use of the back and limbs.

2   *Level*—Three levels at which movement may occur can be

recognized—close to the base of support, far away from the base of support, and an area between the two.

The majority of activities are originated at one of these levels. If an activity is attempted at another level a change will take place in the way the body is used.

3 *Shape*—The shape of the body is closely allied to function. A ball or curved shape results from curling, a narrow shape and a wide or spiky shape from stretching, an angular shape from bending, and a screw-like shape from twisting.

Maintaining a basic activity while changing the shape will result in many new derivations. Investigation into the shape of the body during preparatory and landing movements may result in interesting use of 'body-parts' and suggest new directions in sequence work. Thoughtful attention may be given to the effect of stretching and curling on the speed of rotation of the body.

4 *Extensive or limited use of space*—This refers to the amount of personal and general space occupied. 'Extensive' refers to the expansion of the body and the extent of the pathway of movement.

'Limited' refers to the contraction of the body and the constricted pathway of movement.

Practising an activity with this factor in mind will once again lead to differing use of the body.

New environment

1 *Apparatus*—A simple transfer of the activity from the floor to the apparatus will stimulate variation without further explanation from the teacher, the problem being one of negotiation. The children travel over, along, through, around, or underneath the apparatus, or use a combination of these activities. The variation in surface, in height, in type and size of support, will dictate changes in the basic activity.

Certain activities, e.g. sliding and dropping, which are necessarily limited when practised at floor level, may be developed on the apparatus. The sensation of flight is stimulated and is extended in, or added to, the activity. All the basic activities except hanging, swinging, and climbing, may be practised on the floor before moving on to the apparatus.

The other factors, parts of body, function, and path of movement, can all be used in conjunction with the apparatus. Each in turn will provide a new experience, and skilful use of the body will be acquired.

2 *Group*—The group may consist of two, three, or more members. Cooperating with others in a group will suggest many variations resulting from changing relationships: matching or copying; together or following; contrasting through direction, shape, etc.; mirroring with the consequent use of both sides of the body; meeting and parting in different ways; passing around, over, under or along; supporting or handling.

C QUALITATIVE FACTORS

The motion factors are stressed to develop quality. The teacher helps the child to appreciate the way in which these factors are being used by asking for clarification of time, weight, space, and flow, during the performance of an activity. Understanding of the way in which a factor *is being used* provides the means of developing quality and not by finding *different ways* of demonstrating a factor.

It should also be noted that the quantitative factors, the 'movement variables', are placed first. Although educational gymnastics cannot be taught without bringing out the presence of the motion factors, they should not be stressed as an aspect of teaching until the child's movement vocabulary has been enlarged. After this the motion factors may be stressed to enrich and improve rather than change the activity.

ACTIVITY RECORD CHART

The list of activities at the side of the chart and the quantitative and qualitative factors forming the headings, provide the teacher with a means of systematically covering the programme. An attempt has been made to place them in a logical order although it is appreciated that movements under all these headings are closely related and will be mingled in the practice of any one basic activity. The way in which the chart is used is left to the discretion of the teacher; he could for example merely note the date in the appropriate panel leaving room for further additions. The chart could move through the school with the class so that one can see at a glance the extent of experience of the class. If an additional record is thought necessary a card could be kept for each basic activity and information transferred from the chart to the cards.

This system is intended as a guide to the teacher who is new to the subject, but may be used to advantage by the more experienced teacher to assess whether he is presenting a balanced programme.

CHAPTER SIX

The Senior Phase of Gymnastics

When the secondary school gymnastic programme has progressed into the qualitative phase the method by which it is continued is very dependent on the preferences of the teacher. The following alternatives are available:

1   To continue with educational gymnastics.
2   To continue with a modified form of educational gymnastics in which the programme is supplemented with the skills of Olympic gymnastics.
3   To progress from a democratic approach to the teaching of gymnastics by more direct teaching methods.
4   To use the gymnastic period for specialization. The children will select a subject in which they wish to specialize and the period is used for training purposes. The subjects usually offered are gymnastics, soccer, rugby, basket-ball, and cross-country. The lesson becomes more of a club activity than a teaching period and individual programmes are the basis of the work.
5   To discontinue the teaching of gymnastics in lesson time but to carry it on as a club activity in evening and lunch-time sessions.

ATTITUDE TO SENIOR GYMNASTICS
If the senior boys do very little gymnastics this will have a retarding effect on the achievements of the lower school. Gymnastics should be of prestige value throughout the school.

It should be a recognized form of recreation which is worthy of demonstration to parents, to visitors, and to other schools. It should possess an element of competition which can be displayed at the top level. Gymnastics should be considered as a form of recreation and not solely as training. Admittedly, most of our lives are spent attempting to use our bodies skilfully in a non-recreative way, and it is hoped that the gymnastic lessons help to attain this. The *teacher* may take the development and extension of personal bodily skill and experience as the main objective, but the *child* needs to appreciate and enjoy gymnastics as recreation if he is to retain interest in it.

PROBLEMS OF DIVERGING SKILL

At fourteen years the two ends of the class are drawing further apart and teaching becomes increasingly more difficult. The gross motor skills have been developed and the fundamental gymnastic activities are being extended into more complex skills. The interests of the individual become more forceful and rise above, and out of, general class interest. The field of gymnastic activity is wide and the sensations experienced through these activities are so different that individuals tend to want to do more of this and less of that.

The teacher may find difficulty in selecting a class theme for he is asked to guide the individual more and more. It is not so often possible to stop the whole class and develop a point which is of general application. This stage has passed. Stimulation of thought, coaching, and demonstration, which gives insight into the performance of an activity is often applicable only to one individual, or to a small group who want to improve the same activity.

The traditional gymnastic skills come back into favour for the fourteen-year-old but are developed by the individual as answers to tasks. Those who wish to perform an arab-spring or an overswing may need, and will often ask for, direct coaching in order to improve their skill and widen their knowledge. The desire for mature status which skilled performance can bring to the adolescent requires that vaulting and agility skills be included as an aspect of bodily skill for those who are ready and willing to learn them.

AIMS AND ACHIEVEMENTS

At the senior stage there cannot be a class-teaching approach of this or of that nature. Cooperation is the key word and the function of the teacher is to prepare the situation and supply the encouragement and knowledge so that the pupil acquires the desired result. Individual relationships are all important for it is the adolescent who will decide whether he wishes to experiment with movements and variations, or whether he would prefer to be shown the technique of an activity. He is now capable of extended periods of practice. Early success is not necessary as long as the possibility of achievement in the future is fairly certain. He is prepared to tackle a skill and work at it for a number of weeks before finally gaining success. When this long-term determination to learn can be seen in action, a vitally important educational hurdle has been passed and interest in gymnastics and in other fields of physical education should flourish.

As the senior scheme is dominated by individual attainment and interest the lesson is difficult to plan. It is determined by the reaction of the pupils. The sensible approach would seem to be one that progresses towards selection of apparatus by the teacher but the pupils' choice of an objective is stimulated more by the apparatus than by the teacher. Faced with a group of apparatus a pupil should be encouraged to think of what he can already do, how he can vary this and make it more demanding, and how he can learn something new.

DEVELOPMENT OF APPEAL

The apparatus work has progressed from a task which imposes a general limitation on all the apparatus to one of the following:

1 two or three groups of apparatus are limited in the same way and the remaining groups each have a specific task,
2 each group of apparatus has a different task,
3 free choice of the activity to be practised.

At the start of a term and half-term a new lay-out of apparatus may be planned and tried out for one lesson. The possibilities of successful development and the reaction of the class are then assessed. In Lesson Two the apparatus could be adjusted until the teacher is satisfied that it has appeal and will stimulate the type of activity desired. This arrangement of apparatus is left until the standard of performance of the class is satisfactory, and then gradual progression to new combinations is made by adding to, or rearranging, a group at a time. Sufficient time for repetition of activities must be allowed so the apparatus plan should not be disturbed too frequently.

As the task is applicable only to a specific group of apparatus, it is possible to progress by varying the height, the direction, by adding more apparatus, or by changing the combination. Finally different, and progressively more advanced, tasks could be tackled. It will be necessary to vary the task, or the degree of imposition, according to the ability of the boys working on the apparatus. A specific practice may be given to the more talented which differs from the task attempted by the remainder of the group. There is still danger, however, in attaching too much prestige value to the attainment of the traditional skills. Attention should not be drawn to levels of work or to competitive standards based on *degree of difficulty*. This will tend to discourage the gymnast who is not capable of the difficult activities but who is performing his sequences perfectly well. It may also force the achievement of selected activities at the expense of quality of control in many situations. The arrangement of the class may move towards ability groups but this should happen as naturally as possible and without emphasis.

During the previous phases the arrangement of the apparatus was usually specified by the teacher. At the senior phase the following are possible:

1 The boys choose on which group of apparatus to practise. When the objective of the practice has been reached and a satisfactory quality attained they may move to another group

of apparatus at will. This method is theoretically good but can lead to purposeless drifting from one apparatus to another. The pupil must stay with a piece of apparatus until he has achieved something worthwhile.

2 The arrangement of a group of apparatus is changed as the sequences evolve. New formations may be desirable when the work involves group cooperation.

3 Small apparatus, such as hoops, benches, and mats, is added to the larger apparatus. This may create more interest by increasing the variety and number of movements included in a sequence. Better use of floor space around the major item of apparatus may be stimulated, giving alternative starting and finishing positions and variation in the use of direction. Small apparatus helps to discourage long approach runs followed by a single activity.

4 The wall bars are included as a part of the apparatus. An involved floor pattern sometimes results which needs careful selection and timing of activities to give a natural and flowing sequence.

5 Combinations of apparatus are used, such as the box and ropes with trampette, which demand good control but give a satisfying sequence of activity.

6 The boys may choose and arrange the apparatus on which they wish to work and decide by discussion:
   (a) a group task within the ability of the whole group,
   (b) individual tasks related to their ability,
   (c) a group performance which combines the two.

IMPORTANCE OF VARIETY OF APPARATUS

The amount of portable apparatus available makes a vast difference to the success of the senior work. The sequences are restricted and the difficulty decreased if only three pieces of vaulting apparatus are in use. One really needs two boxes, two horses, a buck, and a set of parallel bars, so that a piece of vaulting apparatus may be included in each group. A trapeze, rings, and vertical and diagonal ropes and ladders increase the challenge of sequence work. Two trampettes, two springboards, and a trampoline should be considered essentials rather than luxuries. If the apparatus is to stimulate adventurous activity then it must be challenging and there must be enough of it to make every group interesting.

IMPORTANCE OF GROUP ACTIVITY

At senior level, gymnastics must not be a lesson where the individual trains 'by himself' to improve his performance. Opportunity must be given for the individual to combine with others in the production of a group sequence. *Group production* is an essential element of the work. A group of three to five works on a gymnastic theme and produces a demonstration of inter-dependent sequence work which has an appeal comparable with an excerpt from drama, dance production, or a well executed move on the soccer field. The pupils find these group productions a most satisfying form of gymnastics, which brings maximum mental and physical effort from *everyone* in the group, no matter what his ability.

Pair activities and group combinations from the earlier lessons in which simple sequences were timed, matched, mirrored, and contrasted, are gradually extended and developed into more demanding and vigorous performances. Examples of themes which may be given to a group to develop are as follows:

1 Horse, buck, springboard, three mats.
   Work with a partner to show a sequence of two jumps, a roll, and a bridge. One boy must pass under the other at a point in the sequence.
2 Ropes, double beam, two benches, three mats.
   The whole group to work together to produce a demonstra-of gymnastics which includes a jump, an upside-down movement, and a balance, by each member. The group must start, finish, and balance at the same time.
3 Box, two benches, wall bars, trampette, four mats.
   Produce a sequence of activity which lasts for one minute on

a theme of leaping and twisting. Demonstrate assisted flight during the sequence.

4 Parallel bars, two benches, four mats.

Each member of the group to develop a sequence consisting of three activities which show how the body weight can be balanced, transferred, and supported by the hands during locomotion. The sequences are then to be performed together so that the group may be seen working together, alternately and in pairs.

These suggestions are very general, and really it is impossible to generalize about adolescents. The presentation of the senior phase must depend on the reaction of the pupils to the teaching of the whole scheme of gymnastics.

CHAPTER SEVEN

Determination to Learn

The text would not be complete without mention of the *attitude* of the child to the learning situation.

Determination to learn covers only one facet of the child's reaction to gymnastics but is of particular importance to the teacher in assessing the quality of the class–teacher relationship. Educators have stressed that the way we teach is as important as what we teach; that it is the way the child learns and his attitude to learning that is important to future progress and not the present standard of skill achieved.

An important objective of educational gymnastics is to increase the ability to *learn* a physical skill. He must think about what he is doing and understand *how* to improve his performance. He should develop the ability to understand the teacher's request, to resolve his own interpretation of the problem, to concentrate and apply real effort to his practice, and finally to present a movement answer which shows the limit of his capabilities.

DETERMINATION TO SUCCEED

For learning to take place, a task must be tackled with determination. It is not possible to originate movements and improve performance if a sense of purpose and a strong desire to accomplish does not accompany the practice. The teacher should help the class to attack a problem with determination and physical effort. He cannot make a child produce physical effort but can encourage him to want to succeed in accomplishing a task involving strength and vigour and toil. He can, by his attitude and method of presentation, enable a child to learn concentration and determination.

Having previously stressed the importance of a feeling of achievement for every child in the class, consideration should be given to the alternative. A teacher must recognize that an end-product of his teaching could also be failure. It is not often possible to gain success for every child, no matter how carefully balanced the material with the range of ability of the class. Is failure part of the learning process, and to what extent is it an experience necessary during physical education?

It seems likely that an older child can learn as much about himself from failure as he can from success. The ability to accept a failure and continue with the practice or work out another method of approach is an essential ingredient of determination. There are times during life when every individual will have to recognize an unsuccessful performance, accept his own lack of ability and, it is hoped, benefit from this experience. He must develop the strength of character to meet and accept failure.

For gymnastics to be worthwhile there must be a higher rate of success than failure for every child. The initial approach of some children to a new experience may be apprehensive. They may be asking themselves if they are capable of tackling the task. If each time, the same group answer that they cannot do it, then failure will result in a decrease in interest and an undermining of determination. If this situation arises it is probably the result of a badly prepared programme. A new learning problem should be based on previous success. Progress from the known to the unknown, from the general to the specific, is applicable to this situation. For a sense of determination to develop, the tasks presented must be graded in difficulty so that the early efforts bring success, and achievement and progress are possible. This progress must from time to time demand more effort, concentration, and perseverance so that difficulties are met and conquered. The individual should not be protected from failure by decreasing the difficulties of tasks, but should be challenged by difficult situations within his capabilities.

The child is generally, though not always, the best judge of his capabilities and he should face each gymnastic situation with a feeling of adequacy. If the task is obviously too difficult he will not try to succeed. He has no feeling of failure or of inadequacy from this; he will probably treat the situation as rather ridiculous, as he does not expect success. If the task is too simple, he will treat it with similar contempt. The problem is to select tasks which are suitable for the range of ability of the whole class and which demand a reasonable amount of effort from every individual. If the child can see his past achievements and is prepared to work for future progress then determination may arise out of the learning situation. It is hoped that he will be able to transfer this ability to other situations involving problems in physical skill.

CHAPTER EIGHT

Organization

If this text is to be helpful to the teacher it must include advice on the organization concerned with gymnastic lessons. Many students and teachers do not give sufficient thought to the storage and movement of apparatus and to changing-room procedure. This is really a fairly straight-forward task and should present no problems. Each class should at first follow a set routine and when sensible habits have been formed they should be given the opportunity to organize the lesson with a minimum of teacher control.

A Organization of Apparatus

When considering the movement of apparatus there is one criterion—efficiency. In the beginning the pupils should be trained in moving and assembling the apparatus. Have one method for each piece of apparatus and organize all carrying operations formally at first, even regimentally. A routine is necessary in order to gain maximum working time and a continuation of the learning atmosphere built up during the floor work. It also ensures complete safety to those carrying the apparatus, to others moving about, and to the apparatus and the floor.

The drills of handling and assembling, and the set formalities of group places, will facilitate the organization and give a feeling of security to child and teacher. The following methods are suggested:

BEAMS

Two pupils using the ropes; another to support the boom. The one pulling the rope should ensure that the top of the boom has travelled all the way along the track and has banged into place. The bolts are then fastened into the floor sockets by the pupil steadying the boom. The pupil holding rope number two brings down the beam and the support pins are placed in and drop-ends checked. Do not use wedges unless balance work is included and then do not allow these to be hammered in.

ROPES

Two pupils detailed, one to operate the pulley rope and the other to prevent the climbing ropes from swinging as they move out. Fasten the pulley rope tightly to the wall hook.

WINDOW LADDER

A pupil should be at each end and one in the centre. Unbolt, lift, and push out from behind. When the top supporting runner has dropped into place, bolt into floor.

BENCHES

To be carried by one person at each end, facing each other. Never allow only one to carry it as the ends will be swung around and the knees of others may be damaged.

BOX

Two to lift the top two sections and two for the bottom three. Latter to be placed on the floor first. One person at each end if the box is on wheels and do not allow anyone to ride on the release bar.

BUCK

Two people facing each other to carry or push. Teach correct method of adjusting length of leg, i.e. one person on each side: A holds the buck towards him while B operates the pins on his side, B then pulls back towards his chest while A adjusts.

HORSE

As above; four people if lifting is necessary, and if they are small.

AGILITY MAT

To be stored tightly rolled and strapped. A stick through the centre is best for carrying by small pupils, or use the linked-hand method.

LANDING MAT

Two or four people, depending on the weight of the mat; carry holding the sides or handles. Refrain from doubling or rolling rubber mats, particularly for storage, and do not allow them to be dragged across the floor. Store with clean surfaces together.

CLIMBING APPARATUS AND FRAMES, WALL BARS, SWING BEAMS

As the type varies the teacher should work out the safest method of assembly by a twelve-year-old and teach this method to all.

STORE ROOM

The storage of the large apparatus is sometimes a problem. Careful thought should be given to the permanent storage positions of the portable apparatus, considering access, weight, size, and amount of use. Mark the floor round the edge of each piece to ensure that the apparatus is returned to its correct site. It may be preferable to store some of the vaulting apparatus, benches, or agility mats, in the corners of the gymnasium where it is easily accessible, than to have it hidden away in a narrow store where movement out is a slow and difficult process and demands teacher supervision. This of course decreases the floor space and creates difficulties when the gymnasium is also used for basketball, games training, and dancing. In this case the teacher is advised to place the apparatus round the walls as near as possible to where it is going to be used, *before* the lesson starts. Attempt to plan the layout of the group apparatus so that the heavy apparatus is used close to the place of storage. The flow of the lesson, and sometimes class control, may be ruined by involved lifting and carrying.

This section on handling of apparatus has been laboured and much may seem trivial, and certainly common sense, but apparatus is often maltreated. The advantages of a routine, particularly for the first-year classes, should be stressed.

B Organization of the Class

Organization in the lower school should be done formally, by a direct 'word-of-command' approach. This is not part of the democratic presentation of material. The following traditional routine is still preferred as the most successful method by which a teacher may organize his class in a gymnasium.

INTRODUCTORY ACTIVITY

When small apparatus is to be used it should be brought out by the first of the class to enter the gym. It is therefore an advantage to store the small balls, ropes, bean bags, etc., in wire containers. The centre of the gymnasium is suggested as the dispersal point so that access from all sides is possible and the teacher has a clear view of what is happening. Never allow the whole class to collect apparatus; this creates disciplinary problems and leads to untidiness. After the activity the apparatus is replaced tidily in the container and one or two of the class detailed to return it to its correct place. Remember that continuity of work is essential, 'Fold your rope into four and tie a knot in the middle. Put it into the container *and* do so and so . . . '

FLOOR WORK

The organization is simple:

If no apparatus is used, the pupils merely spread out sensibly. If hoops or ropes are used, then they should also have been used for the introductory activity so that no additional organization is necessary and teaching may contiue smoothly.

If mats or benches are to be used:

(*a*) tell the pupils to stand close together in groups of three or four,

(*b*) stand on the perimeter where you can see the whole of the class,

73

(c) detail pupils, e.g. two from each group, to carry the apparatus,

(d) first pupils to carry apparatus to positions furthest from place of storage.

When the floor work is finished the teacher directs the apparatus to be kept for the group work to its next position and the remainder to its place of storage.

GROUP APPARATUS WORK

The groups and group places should be permanent. Each group should always stand on the same line on the perimeter of the gymnasium and should bring out and put away the same pieces of apparatus.

1 *Group places*

The groups move into position and stand still, away from the wall bars and apparatus. Teacher should adjust the numbers if necessary. Explain any changes in the assembly of the apparatus.

2 *Apparatus out*

Certain groups should be trained to move their apparatus first, e.g. groups using apparatus kept at the entrance of the store or those carrying apparatus to the far end of the gymnasium. The apparatus should be moved efficiently and sensibly, not necessarily quickly.

3 *Assembly completed*

The boys move back to their group place and should sit or stand still and quiet, and listen.

During the first three stages the teacher should stand by the equipment store where the whole of the class can be seen. Operations are easily directed from this strategic position; do not mix in with the class and help with the carrying and assembling, they must learn to do it themselves. If a group is having difficulty stop them and if only a minor adjustment is necessary help them when movement from the store has finished. If the adjustment will take time (e.g. beam weight off) then make the group wait until the remainder of the class are working on the tasks, then remedy the fault or change the piece of apparatus. Do not keep the whole class waiting.

Quickly check the apparatus for correct positioning and safety. Check the beams, the landing mats (particularly if they have to be secured under the edge of vaulting apparatus to prevent sliding), inclined or double benches, the wheels on vaulting apparatus, and all bolting devices.

4 *Explanation of Tasks*
The ease or difficulty of this will depend on the lesson content. The teacher may:
(a) give a free choice of activity on the apparatus,
(b) give a task which covers every group and can be explained in one sentence,
(c) give a task which covers five or six groups and explain separate tasks for the remaining two or three groups,
(d) give a separate task to each group. This is the difficult method, particularly for a student having a class for the first time. Go to each group in turn and introduce the task by a very *short* explanation. Make sure that you talk to the whole class and not to one group. Make sure they can all hear and are listening. Make a point of asking a question of someone in a distant group. Make sure also that they are paying attention and can see any demonstration. Move some of the groups if necessary. When the explanations are completed each group should know what to do on the apparatus. When they change apparatus they should not have to ask what to do on the new apparatus.

5 *Start Work*
After the time allowed for the first group practice, the groups should be moved to the next apparatus, formally at first, and by varying methods as they progress. The formal method is stop! move to the next position; start work.
The pause while waiting to move gives an opportunity for

class control, a demonstration by a group with points emphasized by the teacher, or the addition of a limitation to a task.

6 *Apparatus away*

Groups return to their permanent place and put away the apparatus they assembled. Apparatus to be returned to the back of the store should be moved first.

Advice to the College Student

ROUTINE

The student on teaching practice is advised to follow this type of routine until he feels confident that the organization is running smoothly, and he is in complete control. The drills may be relaxed and shortened when the boys are experienced in handling the apparatus correctly and have developed self-discipline. It is very likely that the class–teacher already has a routine working which differs from the above. The student should make use of the known routine and not try to change it unless response is unsatisfactory. However, 'This is what they are used to', is not an acceptable excuse for lack of organization.

PRESENTATION

The student also has the difficult task of taking over the teacher's plan of apparatus, activities, and a method of presentation which may be foreign to his beliefs and training. Is he to ensure continuity of the work as far as is sensible, or attempt a complete change of attitude and approach?

DIRECTION AND DISCIPLINE

For the experience he should try to teach educational gymnastics but should do so only with the teacher's permission. One cannot gain full appreciation of the value of the work when the class has a previous history of formal teaching; the class will tend to be lost when offered a thought-provoking choice of activity. They will wait to be told what to do and when the instructions are not given may resort to playground activities and look upon the lack of direction and domination as weakness on the part of the teacher. In a few years' time, however, the democratic method of teaching gymnastics may be the rule in secondary education rather than the exception. In the preliminary visit to the school the following information should be collected:

1 the lesson framework used,
2 method of presentation,
3 method of organization,
4 a plan of the last lesson giving position of the apparatus used, the tasks in progress, and the floor work,
5 plan of gymnasium showing fixed apparatus,
6 portable and small apparatus available.

This information gives the background for lesson preparation and if possible should be coupled with observation of a lesson to give some idea of the best method of presentation to adopt and the type of response to be expected.

The student may return from the preliminary visit without information to help in lesson preparation. Questions may receive responses such as:

'Take what you like.'
'I do very little gymnastics but would like you to try some.'
'Never mind what I've been doing. Let's see you do it your way.'
'I do circuit training.'
'The P.E. man is not available today.'

In this case, report back to the P.E. tutor who will help to plan an experimental lesson suitable to the age-group. He may be able to base it on his experience of the school.

When a new layout of apparatus is used for the first time it is wise to spend the majority of the lesson on the group apparatus section. There are two alternatives for Lesson One:

(*a*) Introductory Activity   or   (*b*) Introductory Activity
    Running Sequence   Apparatus Work
    Floor Work

Alternative (*a*) is theoretically the best as it gives an easier start and produces a floor sequence which can be used on the apparatus in Lesson Two. Alternative (*b*) gets the difficult task of organizing the apparatus over in the first lesson and leaves the way clear for good results in Lesson Two. This may be an advantage as tutors tend to keep away from first lessons but expect to see progress in Lesson Two.

C Organization of Changing

Many of the difficulties and disciplinary problems of physical education arise in non-working time. It is very important to establish standards of behaviour in the changing room. This is top priority in the organization of P.E.

The following points may prove helpful when planning the changing routine:

1 Where does the class collect—in the classroom, corridor, outside the gym, or inside the changing room? It is advisable to go to meet the younger boys and instil good habits. Control from the source is better than starting with a noisy gathering in the changing area. Control the class quietly but firmly. Use the 'Pause' and the 'Look'. Assess the attitude of the class and react accordingly. Have a calm organized beginning to the lesson and remember that the lesson begins when the teacher and the first boy meet, and *not* five minutes later when you start presenting the lesson material.

2 Be ready for the class on time. Punctuality prevents problems. Do not allow the first-years or any unruly classes into the changing room unsupervised. A trustworthy class who keep to your standards should enter, change, and start work as soon as possible.

3 Have a set drill for the collection of kit from lockers and a permanent peg and place for changing. This will stop the bigger boys from pushing the smaller boys out of 'my place'. Insist that clothes are tidy, ties hung up, socks placed in shoes,

etc., so that no clothing is mislaid. Allow no fooling with clothes as this can spread and cause a serious problem. Make an issue of finding any article that is reported lost and give warning of the consequences of deliberate hiding of clothing, tying knots in ties and braces, and removing shoe laces.

The class should be quiet while changing before the lesson and while the showers are in use. This does not mean *no* talking; be sensible about quietness and silence. Allow more talking and discussion after the lesson as long as they dress quickly.

4 Collect the notes from those who wish to be excused from the lesson and keep a record of their names.

What is to be done with these and the ones who have forgotten their gymnastic kit?

Do not leave them in the changing room. If they are not going into a classroom make them bring work or a book to read, and sit them on a bench at the end of the gymnasium. Do not allow them to sit on the top of the wall bars. They are out of sight. And do not let them talk to boys who are working.

5 Use a 'walk through' drill for the showers and watch them go through. Keep the drying space away from the changing area. Wet children and dry clothes should not come into close proximity.

6 At the end of the lesson they should dress, replace kit if a locker system is used, and sit down to wait until the whole of the class is ready. The class should not leave in ones and twos over a few minutes. This is unfair to the teacher taking the next class. Occasionally follow the class and check that they walk along corridors or across the playground as an orderly group. Dismiss them on time or they will make a habit of arriving late for the next lesson and will blame this on you.

7 A pair of shorts and plimsolls are provided either by the school or by the pupil. Provision by the school causes the most trouble. Being school property, it is kept in lockers in the changing room and an efficient marking system is needed. The plimsolls and shorts should be marked on the outside

directly on to the material if possible. 'Domestos' will bleach a number on to black material. Above each locker have a list which shows compartment number, pupil's name, and numbers on kit.

Compartment	Name	Shorts	Plimsolls
9	Jones, A.	14	27
10	Knowles, T.	17	81

Checking kit is a problem. In their haste boys will take the wrong kit, or replace it in the wrong compartment. A habit routine by the boy of checking the numbers before changing, and a quick locker check by the teacher, before dismissal, is necessary. The locker must be kept locked when not in use. Other classes must not have the opportunity to borrow kit. Unsupervised changing for lunch-time and evening practices can cause trouble and the boys must be trained to feel responsible for the care of their class locker.

When the kit is provided by the boy he is then responsible for its safety and should keep it in his desk, his classroom locker, or at home. Shorts should be of hard-wearing material suitable for gymnastics and games and not of a light colour. Where possible it is preferable to have separate shorts for gymnastics and for games.

The first task of a teacher starting at a school where there is not a standard gymnastic kit in use is to select shorts in the school's colours (or some other suitable colour) and to sell them to the new intake each year. Mark every pair of shorts with the boy's name before he wears them. If he provides a pair of plimsolls mark them clearly. If he does not he will have to work in bare feet, never in socks. Keep a dozen pairs of shorts on hand and lend them to boys who forget their kit when you think the situation demands it, and charge laundry expenses. Some schools now have a laundry attached to the changing rooms area where P.E. clothing is washed regularly. This helps considerably with standards of dress and cleanliness and the kit may then remain in the school for a term.

STANDARDS IN THE GYMNASIUM

The general ability of a P.E. teacher and his overall value to the school may be assessed fairly accurately without even seeing him teach by the standard of gymnastic dress, the number excused P.E. lessons, and changing-room procedure.

If a new teacher has attained a high standard in these three items by the end of his first year of teaching he is well on the way towards success.

Every P.E. teacher worth his salt will expect his gymnasium to receive the same treatment as a classroom, the woodwork room, the science room. He should have pride in the appearance and order of his gymnasium. It is not a playground where the teenager may let off steam by kicking and banging the equipment. The floor and the apparatus need careful treatment or they become dangerous. They should receive the same care and attention as the lathe, the microscope, and the piano.

Do not neglect the smallest item which will lower standards; tape the cracked hoops, plug and tighten loose screws, check apparatus for worn rubber feet, learn how to replace a beam weight, remove dirt from floor sockets, bar all shoes (including the headmaster's) and muddy plimsolls. Take your responsibilities seriously, and the school, pupils, and cleaning staff will respond accordingly.

Conclusion

Gymnastics is initially doing what comes naturally, and at the more advanced levels may progress to doing what comes unnaturally, i.e. finding out how to do things the hard way and testing one's bodily powers. It is based upon the natural rhythm and patterns of human locomotion. Man naturally adapts his locomotion to the circumstances enforced by the environment. He is capable of walking, running, crawling, jumping, rolling, swinging, heaving, etc., as the need arises.

To stimulate the performance of these activities by setting up a gymnastic environment may be artificial, but even after taking the restrictions into consideration gymnastics still gives a wonderful opportunity to experience the pleasure gained from using one's body in skilful and original ways. It is essential to preserve an active interest in the body as the instrument which is used to fulfil one's life, particularly its use in our innate physical abilities. Bodily movement must not be forgotten or taken for granted.

When children enter the secondary school they do not suddenly lose their vast supply of energy and their joy in movement. No change takes place at eleven or twelve years which justifies any change in approach. Interest in the body and its movement potential is still there, and there are a vast range of bodily experiences which need to be added during the secondary stage.

Physical experience must not be curtailed by school routines and environmental demands. The opportunity to satisfy bodily activities within their ability is still very necessary. It is vitally important that a twelve- and thirteen-year-old should continue to find delight in muscular activity. If a genuine appreciation of bodily activity can be fostered and secured by fifteen years of age it is likely to last throughout life. Pleasurable activities which bring a sense of achievement should be channelled into some form of recreation. Progress will lead to specialization by a natural process of selection. Specialization, which is not forced or engineered, should have a lasting effect on life.

Activity Record Chart

Activity List	QUANTITATIVE			DEVELOPMENT						QUALITATIVE DEVELOPMENT			
	Activities	Parts of Body	Function and shape	Level	Direction	Space	Apparatus	Group	Time	Weight	Space	Flow
Walking												
Running												
Hopping												
Jumping												
Landing												
Balancing												
Falling												
Rolling												
Sliding												
Bridging												
Crawling												
Somersault												
Wheeling												
Climbing												
Hanging												
Dropping												
Swinging												
Diving